Cards and Memories to Treasure
Embroidery on paper

Erica Fortgens

CANTECLEER

Contents

Ecstasy Crafts
PO Box 525
Watertown, NY
13601 USA

Ecstasy Crafts
630 Shannonville Rd
Shannonville, ON
KOK 3AO Canada

Toll free 888-288-7131
Fax 613-968-7876
Email: info@ecstasycrafts.com
Website: www.ecstasycrafts.com

First printed in 2002

ISBN 90 213 3208 6

Publisher: Annemarie Paalvast
Cover: Hans Britsemmer, Kudelstaart
DTP: Cees Overvoorde, Utrecht
Photography: Hennie Raaymakers, St. Michielsgestel
Photography styling: Willemien Mommersteeg, St. Michielsgestel
Drawings: Erica Fortgens
Illustrations: Sjaak van Went, Leiden
Supervision: Sandra Broekhuizen
Translation: Esperanto WBT Arnhem, Arnhem

This book is published by
Uitgeverij Cantecleer
Postbus 309
3740 AH Baarn
The Netherlands

Cantecleer is part of Tirion Publishers bv

Erica Fortgens
Borduren op Papier
Erica Fortgens

Introduction

This is a unique book offering many possible ways for you to make exclusive cards and memory pages for every occasion!

Embroidery on paper is an original technique that enables you to create a personal work of art in a reasonably short period of time. The splendid multi-functional stencils for embossing, cutting and piercing will provide a tasteful result.

This book aims to allow you to use your own creativity; all patterns work on their own, but they can also be used to make cards for any occasion, and you can also use them to freshen up your memory album. The photos show a number of ideas and possibilities, such as weddings, births, Christmas, Thanksgiving, birthdays etc.

If you want to embroider a memory page, it is perhaps a good idea to embroider on a card, which you can then stick into the album; this will make the task somewhat easier.

If you love embroidery, then Embroidery on Paper is a unique opportunity for you to enhance your skills.

Enjoy your hobby!

Erica Fortgens

With many thanks to Leonie Heuyerjans and Anneke Kaufman.

Materials used

- Very fine Erica® piercing tool with accompanying embroidery needle.
- Fine Erica® piercing tool with accompanying embroidery needle.
- Coarse Erica® piercing tool with accompanying embroidery needle.
- Erica® embossing tools in three different sizes.
- Erica® hobby knife
- Erica® cutting ruler
- Erica® piercing pad
- Erica®'s square cards (ideal for embossing)
- Erica®'s rectangular cards (ideal for embossing)
- Erica®'s parchment paper for embossing (for embroidery; also ideal for embossing – no light box needed!)
- A variety of multi-functional stencils are used to help with cutting and embossing, and different piercing patterns are included for elegant piercing and embroidery.
- The square stencils: Decorative, Elegant, Geometrical and Romantic, Allure, Antique and Starlight.
- The rectangular stencils: Passe-partout, Flower and Heart, Victorian, Ornament, Jugendstil, Bethlehem and Party.
- Embossing light box
- Small piece of soap
- Cutting pad
- Double-sided adhesive film
- Glue stick
- Cellotape
- Thread: Sewing machine embroidery thread weight #40. Recommended: Alcazar, Metallic and Reflecta, from Coats. Floss may also be used.

General method

The best sequence to follow for this combination of techniques is:

Piercing- Embossing- Embroidery- Finishing Off

Piercing

Photocopy the required pattern, cut it out neatly, keeping it small, and stick it onto the card or memory page with 2 small pieces of cellotape.

Fold card open and place on piercing pad with front side up.

Pierce all dots carefully with very fine piercing tool. Hold the piercing tool as straight as possible so that clear holes are made. See photo 1.

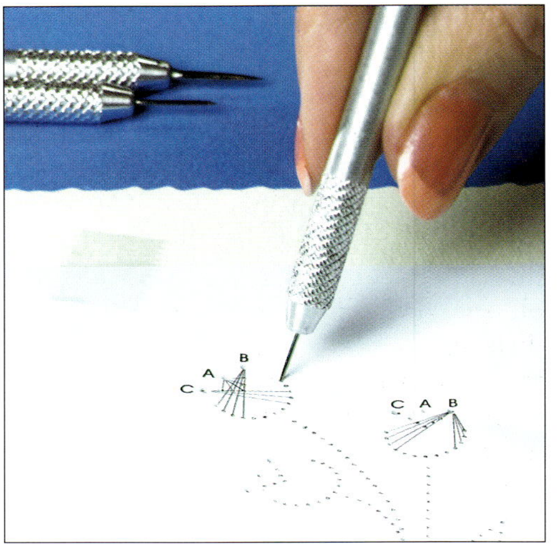

Photo 1

Pierce the larger dots with the coarse piercing tool, making a large hole for multiple threads.

If you make a mistake while piercing the holes, place a small piece of cellotape on the back of the card covering incorrect holes and continue piercing.

Before removing the pattern from the card, hold both up against the light to ensure that all holes in the pattern have been pierced.

TIP

Keep the photocopies in a folder after use; if you have pierced them well you can use them again and again!

Photo 2

The needle

The needle must always be thinner than the piercing tool; use the needle that comes with the piercing tool.

TIP Does your thread become frayed? Rub a very small drop of glue onto the end of the thread; it will dry immediately and keep the thread intact.

Embroidery

Work step-by-step following the instructions for each individual card. Take one strand of thread about 30 inches or 70 cm long or if double thread is desired about 3 feet or 1.30 m. Thread the needle (use needle threader) and pull through until double thread is obtained. Insert needle through pierced hole from the back at the starting point. Leave about 1/2 inch or 2 cm of thread and attach to the back of the card using a small piece of cellotape. See photo 2. Do not cover pierced holes!

Photo 3

Follow instructions for each pattern.

TIP

How to use a needle threader: place the pointed wire tip through the eye of the needle. Now place the single strand of thread through the wire of the needle threader. See photo 3. While holding the needle in one hand, pull the needle threader (hold the wire firmly) and thread back through the eye of the needle. See photo 4.

Photo 4

Various stitches are used. The Flat stitch is a stitch to move from dot to dot. The Stem stitch is used to generate curved lines.

Stem stitch:

Insert the needle from the back at hole 1 and pull thread to hole 2 where needle is put down through the hole. Go along the back to hole 3 and pull thread to hole 4. Go along the back to hole 5 and pull thread to hole 6. And so on as indicated in the diagram skipping two holes on the front each time and one hole on the back.

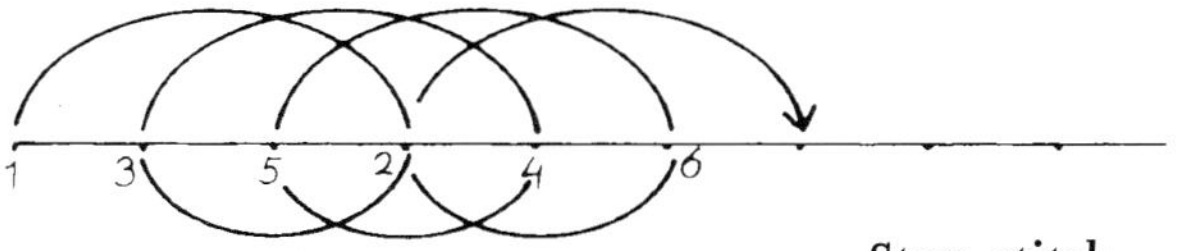

Stem stitch

For small curves skip one hole.

IMPORTANT

Remember to come up on the inside of the curve. Pull away the previous thread with your thumb, in order not to pierce the previous stitch.

TIP

Use sewing machine embroidery thread. This thread is strong and has a lovely sheen. Use a double thread. Note: never use a double thread of Metallic, as this will make it extremely untidy. To create a good finish you can also use a double thread of floss.

TIP

To separate floss: Cut thread to 70 inches or 1.30 m. To separate one strand pull apart the strand a distance, then place the longer end between your knees and hold gently. Holding the one strand in your right hand and the 5 strands in your left, separate the strands by keeping the thread taut and pulling up on the thread allowing it to slip between your knees until fully separated.

TIP

To avoid knotting of the thread: Pull thread trough the card gently and not too quickly. If the thread becomes twisted while working with double threads, let the thread hang down with the needle so it can unravel itself.

TIP

Make sure that the holes that have to be pierced large are in fact large enough; a number of threads may have to pass through them. If a hole does not turn out to be large enough while you embroidery, pierce it again with the coarse piercing tool.

Finishing off

Fold the embroidered card and the cover sheet in half.

Using a glue stick, attach the cover sheet to the back of the card to cover the threads from the embroidery. Glue the cover sheet only to the side where there are threads to cover.

A message or greeting may be placed on the loose back half of the cover sheet.

TIP

When embroidery on Erica®'s Parchment Paper, make sure that you stick the thread on the back as close as possible to the pattern, as the thread will shine through the paper. The best thing to do is stick it tight with a drop of glue (do not make a mess!) on an embroidered section, or weave the thread with the needle back through the stitches already made.

Embossing

Embossing constitutes an important part of this book; there are now 14 different multi-functional Erica® stencils available: see materials

Each stencil is uniquely designed with many patterns woven into the stencil that allow it to be used for many different sized designs using various parts of the stencil. It is the art of leaving out; just pick your choice!

Always make sure that you pierce first, then apply the embossing and then start embroidering: if you embroider first, you cannot emboss any more because of the tape on the back of the card.

Pierce pattern into the card.

Choose the stencil that you wish to use and place it on light box, taping it down using cellotape.

Switch on the light. Place your card FRONT SIDE DOWN on top of the stencil and tape it to the light box.

First use coarse embossing tool to exert light pressure on the paper going to the edges of the stencil, later on use a finer one.

The paper will be raised on the front side of your project according to the stencil used.

Other applications with the stencils

The embossing stencils are also very suitable for stencilling: for this purpose you use a small ink-pad. Cover the rims which you do not use with cellotape.

Trace the borders with a gel pen; this is very effectual on, for instance, dark cards which you cannot emboss.

If you want to emboss on a dark card all the same, you proceed as follows. Place the cards between two identical stencils. Make sure that the stencils fit well when glueing them. Apply the embossing.

TIP

If you use card stock, you will need a light box.
If you use Erica®'s parchment paper for embossing (heavy duty parchment paper), you will not need a light box since the paper is transparent.

TIP

When applying embossing you can rub in the back of the card with a little bar of soap; this makes embossing much lighter and easier!

TIP

The following stencils are ideal to cut with: Geometric, Passe-partout, Allure, Antique, Starlight. Glue the stencil firmly to the card and make any desired cut out. Cut along the opening of the stencil or draw a fine pencil line and then cut. Please note: always cut along the same side of the opening in the stencil: this means that you have to turn the card with the stencil on it over and over again. This yields the best results. Use cutting pad and Erica®'s Hobby knife.

Alphabet

Pull the straight threads from hole to hole. Draw the threads really tight.

If you are going to make your own texts:

Neatly cut out the photocopied letters and use the gluestick to stick them neatly along a pencil-drawn horizontal line on a white sheet of paper.

Figures

Use the stem stitch for the figures.

INSTRUCTIONS ON PAGE 12

80
1922
A
SPECIAL
PERSON

A Special Person

Composition in blue

Stencil used: Decorative

All the patterns of the memory-page can also be applied to a card.

A1. Insert the needle from the back at A and pull threads to the 5 points as shown. Repeat this from B and across this from C. Make the leaves in the same way. Make the stems in the stem stitch.

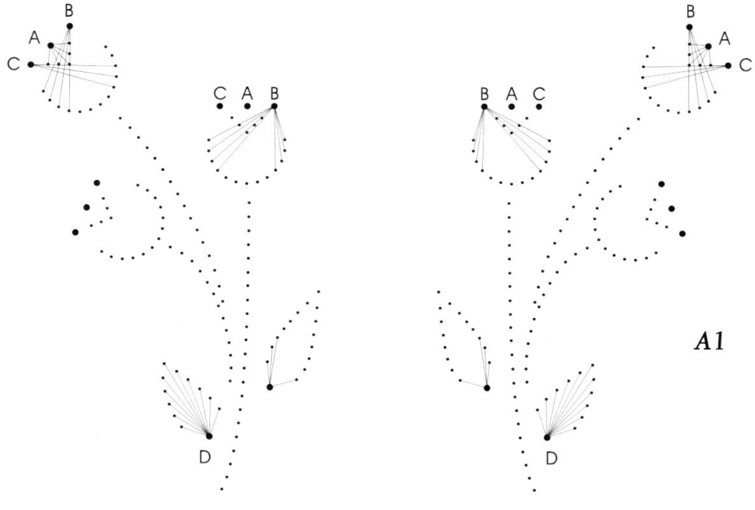

A1

A2. Insert the needle from the back near A and pull threads to the 5 points as shown. Make the leaves in the same way. Use a ribbon to finish off the card.

A3. See A2.

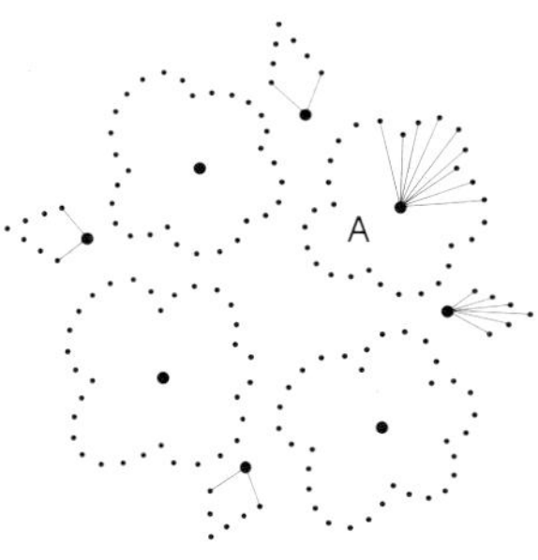

A2

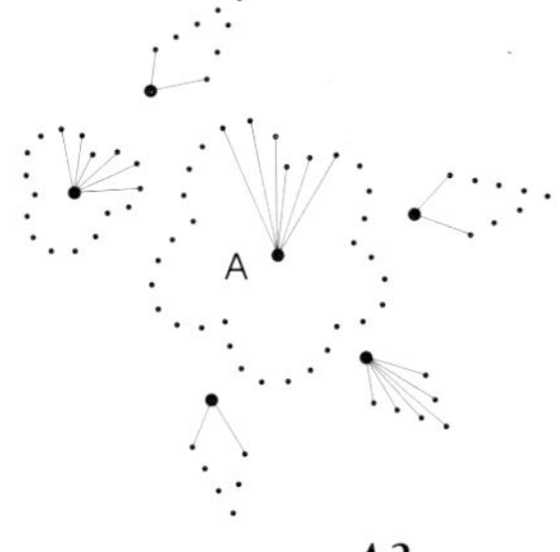

A3

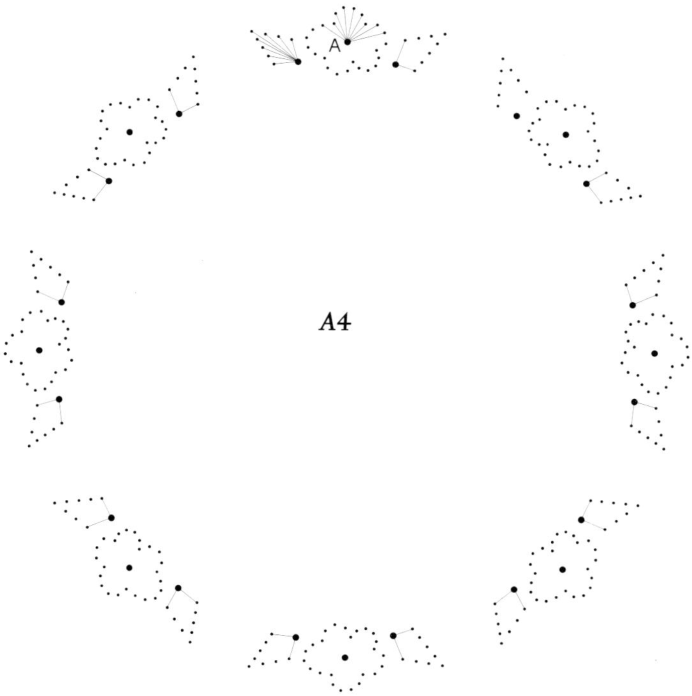

A4

A4. See A2.

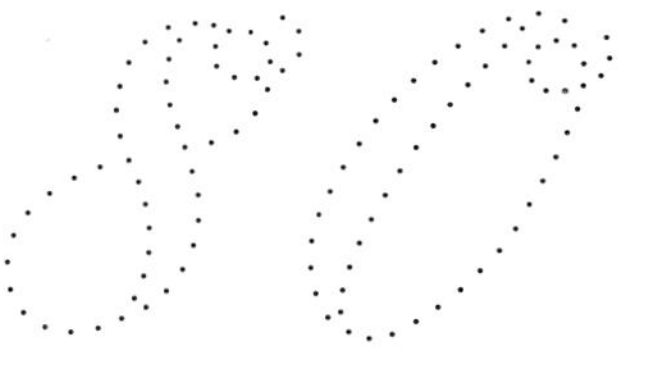

A6

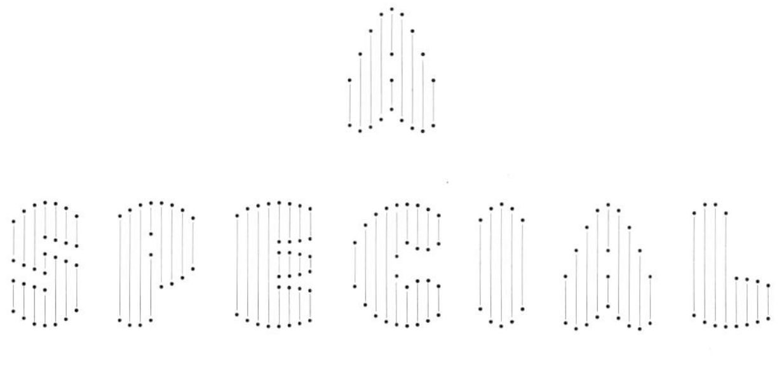

A5

A5. Pull threads from hole to hole. Draw the threads really tight.

A6. Embroider the 80 in stem stitch (see introduction).

Baby Girl

Cards and Memory page in pink

Use stencil: "Flower and heart" and "Elegant"

B1. Embroider the crosses as follows: thread needle from the back at 1 and pull the thread to 2. Go to 3 round the back and pull thread to 4. Go to 5 round the back and pull thread to 6, etc. until you have made the cross. Make the straight stitches of the dress and the decoration at the bottom of the frock. Embroider the face, mouth and hands in stem stitch. Hair: use Ultra Punch or very thin wool. Pierce with piercing tool fine. Insert needle from the back and thread back in same hole. Make a loop. Hold the loop with your thumb while making the next loop. Make the eyes with a bead or a knot in the thread.

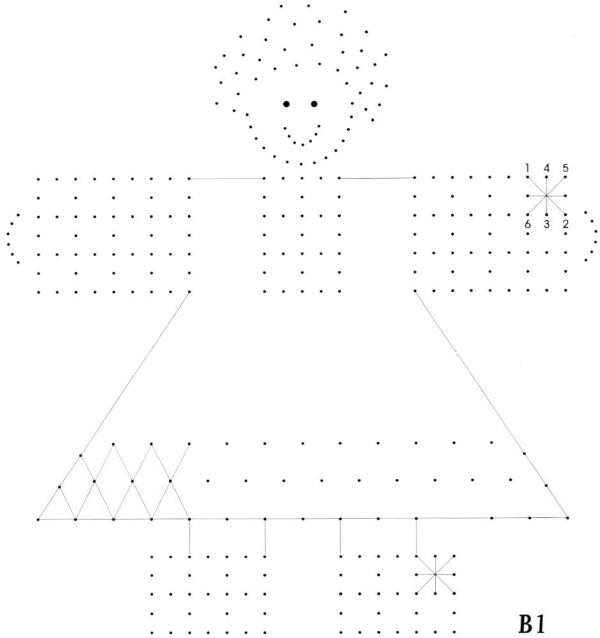

B1

B2. Pull the threads from hole to hole. Draw the threads really tight.

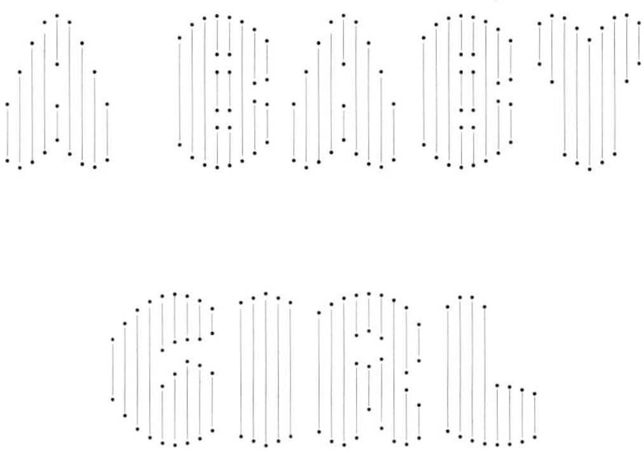

B2

INSTRUCTIONS ON PAGE 14

AMANDA
A BABY
GIRL

B3. Pull the straights threads of the hood of the cradle and the zigzag stitches. Make all round lines in stem stitch.

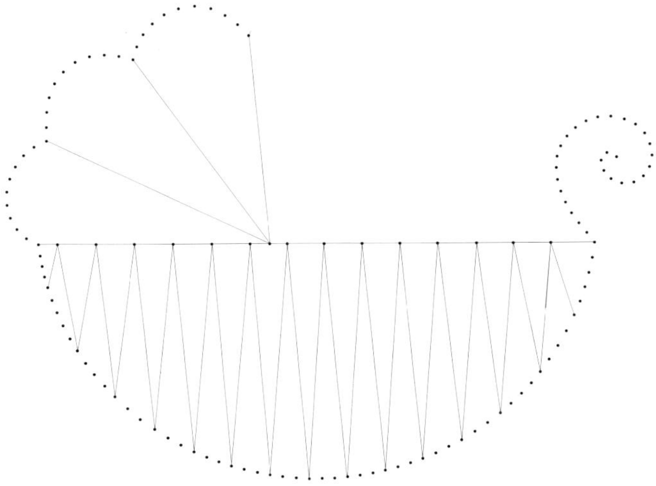

B3

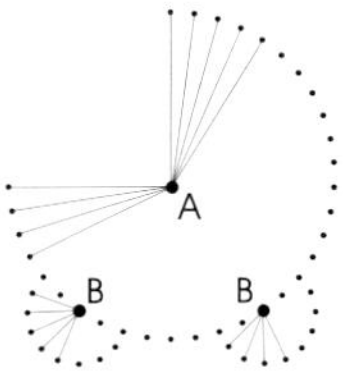

B4

B4. Insert needle from the back at A .(Pierce a very large hole here) and pull threads to all points around. Repeat this at B for the wheels.

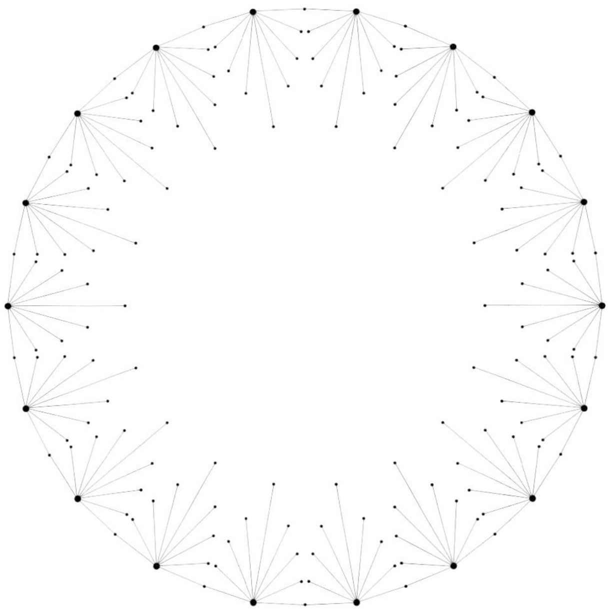

B5

B5. Insert needle from the back at A and pull threads to all points as shown.

Happy Anniversary

Stencil used: Ornament

C1. Embroider the clocks as follows: insert needle from the back at 1 and pull thread to 2. Go along the back to 3 and pull thread to 4. Go along the back to 5 and pull thread to 6, etc., until you have worked round the clock. Pull the straight threads to the top. Flowers and petals: insert needle from the back at A and pull threads to the points as shown. Embroider the bow in stem stitch.

C2. Pull the straight threads from hole to hole. Draw the threads really tight.

C1

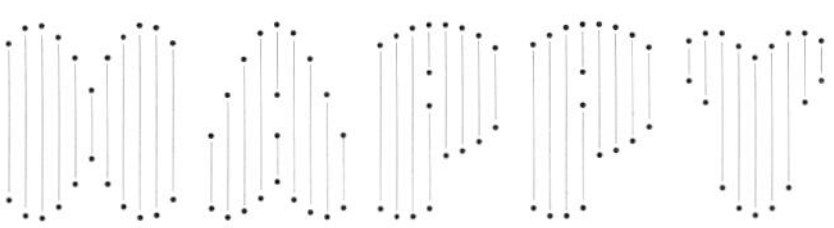

C2

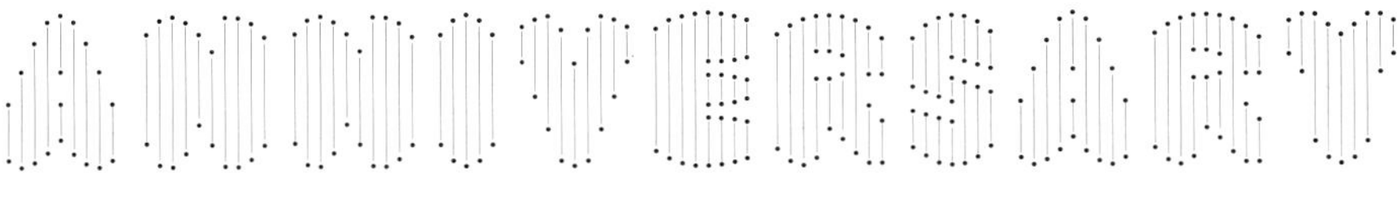

C3. Embroider the figures in stem stitch

C4. Flowers and petals: see C1.

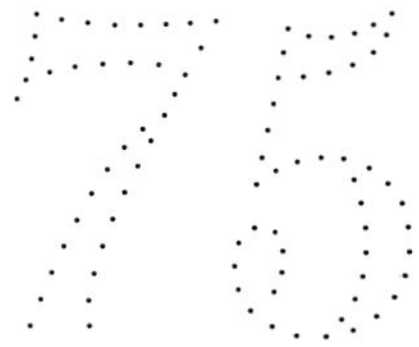

C3

C5. Embroider the figures in stem stitch, embroider the edge as follows: insert needle from the back at 1 and pull thread to 2. Go along the back to 3 and pull thread to 4. Go along the back to 5 and pull thread to 6, etc., until you have worked round the oval. When you have finished embroidering, two threads will stick out in each hole.

C4

C5

Label

The piercing pattern is the top section of pattern C4.

INSTRUCTIONS ON PAGE 17

1-6-1963
HAPPY ANNIVERSARY
75

Our Trip

Holiday page and flower cards

You can use the patterns in this chapter for your Memory-album, but you can also make beautiful birthday or get well cards with them! Insert needle from the back at A and pull threads to the points as shown.

Stencil used: Elegant

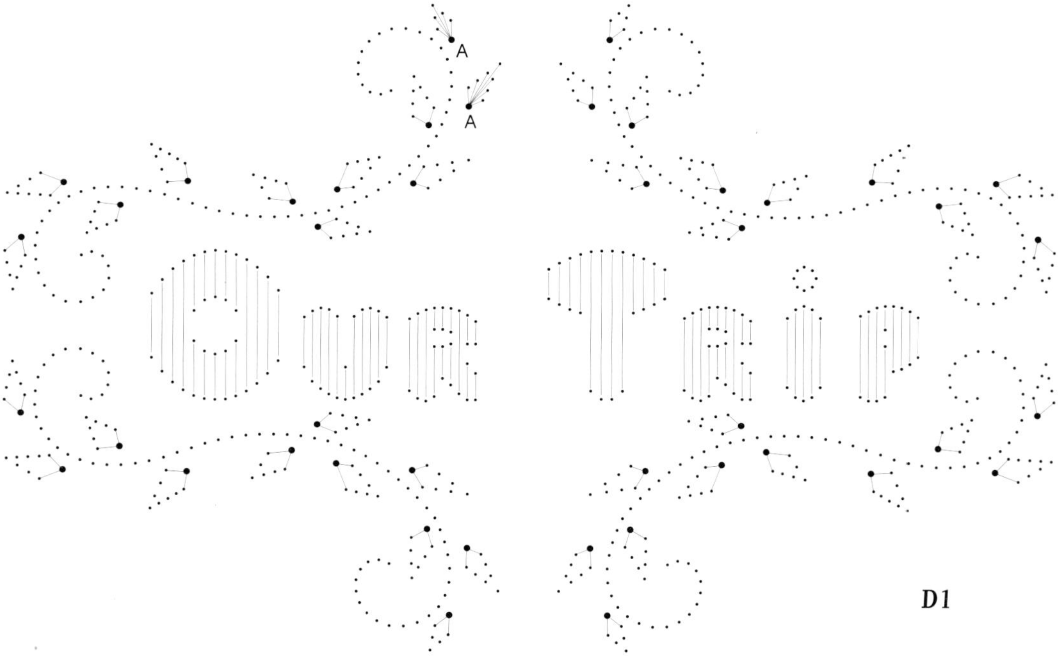

D1

D1. Leaves: insert needle from the back at A and pull needle to all points as shown. Stems: in stem stitch. Our tip: pull straight threads from hole to hole. Draw threads really tight.

D2. Embroider the butterfly in stem stitch. You can add colour to the butterfly with a pastel pencil. Rub out the coloured part somewhat with your finger.

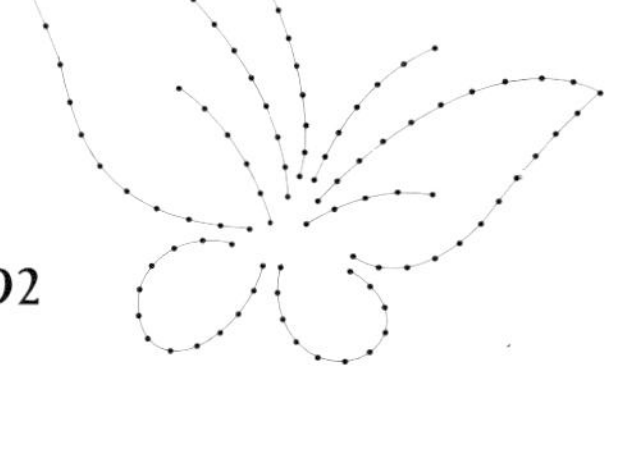

D2

D3

D3. Insert needle from the back at A and pull threads to all points round. Make petals in same way.

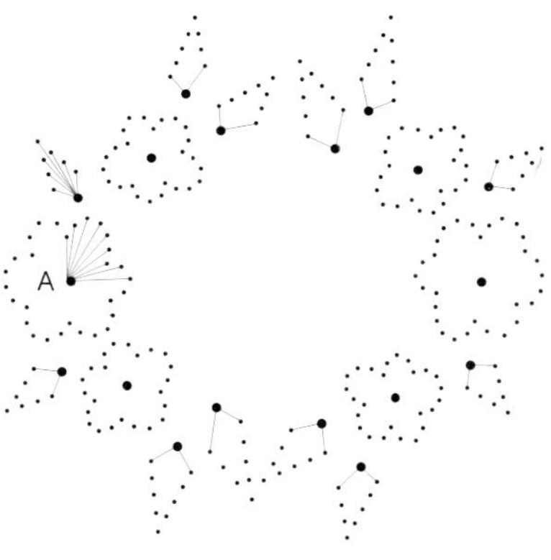

D4

D4. Embroidery: see D3. Embroider on a 5.5 by 5.5 cm card. Stick this on to a piece of parchment paper for embossing: 10 by 10 cm. Stick this again on to a 13 by 13 cm card. Frame the various cards with gold threads. Embroider the butterfly (D2) in stem stitch and add some colouring to it using a pastel pencil. Use 'stamens' for the palps; stick them below the butterfly with a drop of glue.

D5. See D3.

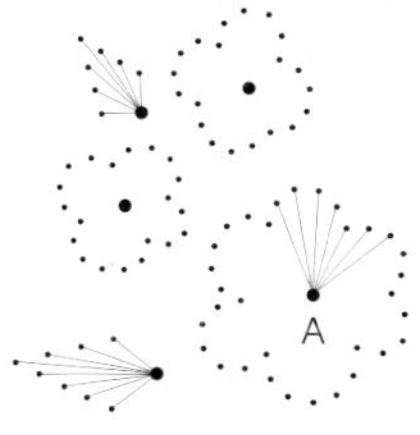

D5

Happy Birthday and God Bless America

Stencil used: "Flower and heart" and "Passe-partout"

E1. Cut a white card size 10.5 x 7.5 cm. Cut a dark blue card size 4 x 3.5 cm. Embroider the stars on the dark blue card. Insert needle from the back at 1 and pull thread to 2. Go along the back to 3 and pull thread to 4, etc, until you have worked round the cross.

E1

Red stripes on the white card: use a double thread red floss. Draw the threads really tight but not too tight, to avoid warping of the card. Insert needle from the back in adjacent hole again and again. Make all the stripes in this way. Stick the dark blue card in its place. Now stick the white card on a dark blue card size 1.5 x 8.5 cm.

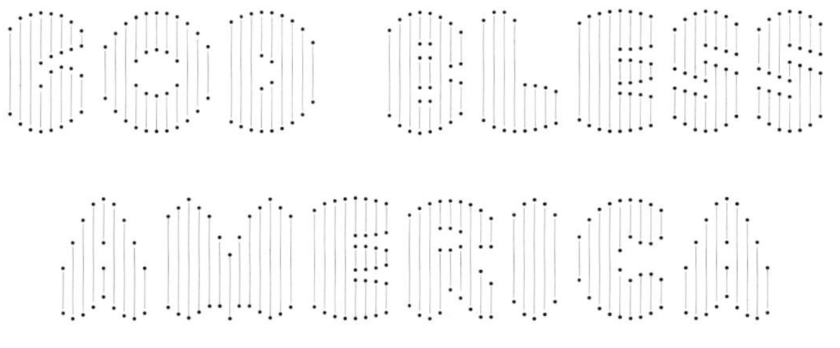

E2

E2. Embroider the letters (pull the threads from hole to hole) on a card, size10.5 x 4.5 cm. Stick this on to a white card, size 1.5 x 6.5 cm, and stick this again on a red card size, 12.5 x 6.5 cm.

INSTRUCTIONS ON PAGE 22 ➤

HAPPY
BIRTHDAY
GOD BLESS
AMERICA

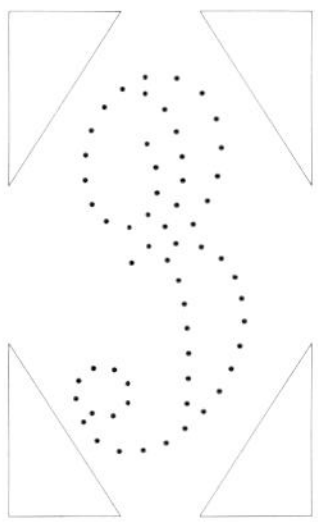

E3

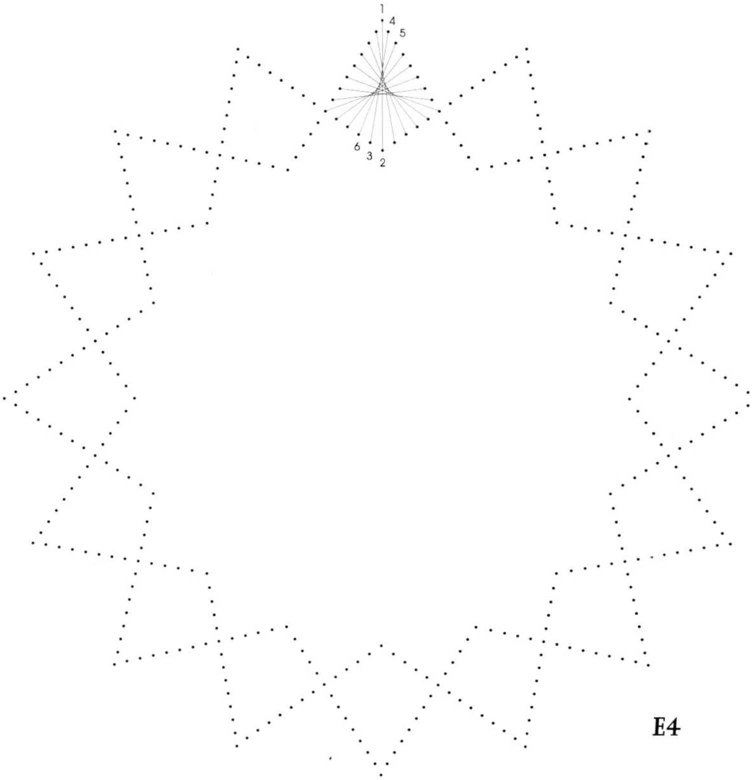

E4

E3. Embroider the figures in stem stitch.

E4. Insert needle from the back at 1 and pull thread to 2. Go along the back to 3 and pull thread to 4. Go along back to 5 and pull thread to 6, etc. until you have worked round the square.

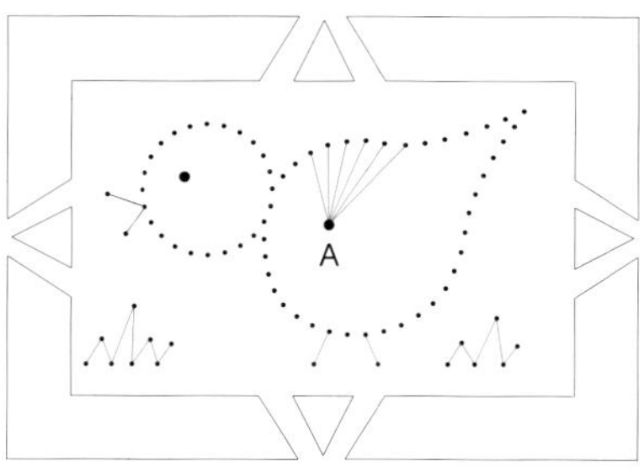

E5

E5. Pierce central holes very large. Insert needle from the back at A and pull threads to all points round. Make head of chicken in the same way. Embroider the legs and mouth in red.

E6. Pierce the holes at A very large. Insert needle from the back at A and pull threads to all points as shown. Embroider the triangles below the balloons and finish the rest of the figure in stem stitch.

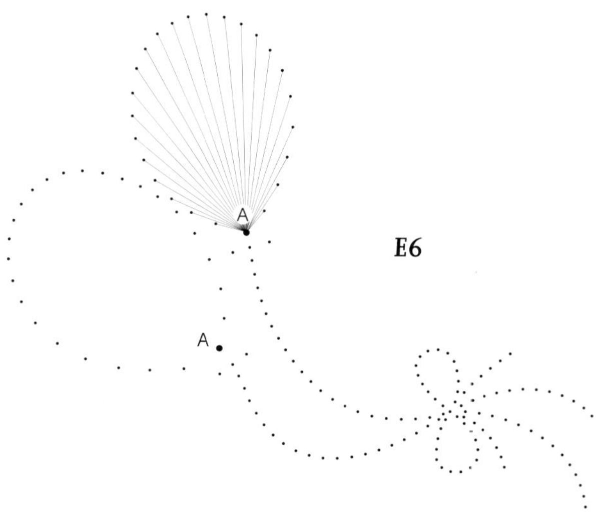

E6

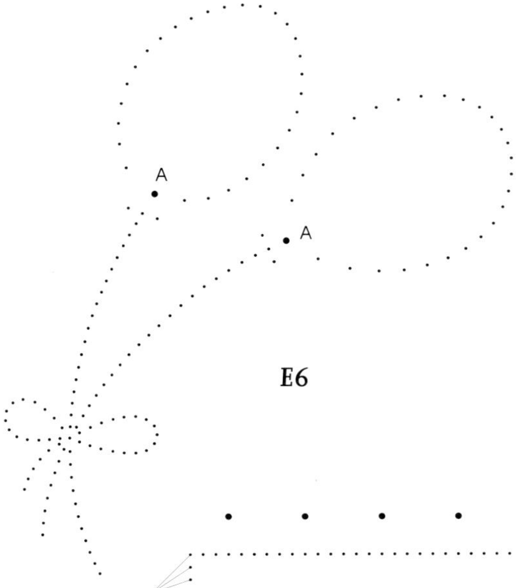

E6

E7. Insert needle from the back at A and pull threads as shown to all points across from A. Pierce the holes at A a bit larger with the piercing tool coarse.

E7

E8. Pull the threads of the letters from hole to hole.

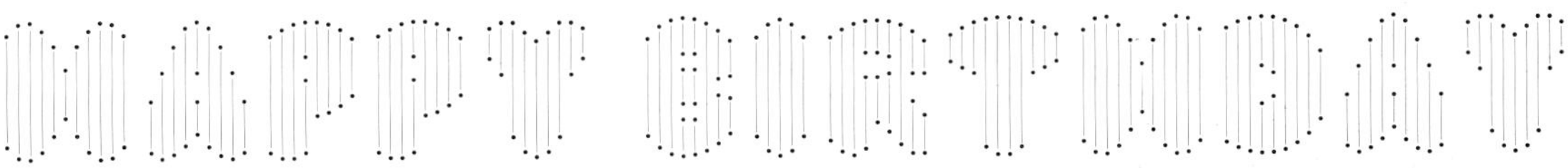

E8

Happy Thanksgiving

Autumn Cards

Stencil used: Elegant and Passe-partout

The patterns in this chapter take a little more time. If you want to make a memory-page, it may be easy to embroider the various embroidery patterns on to cards and stick these in the book.

F1. Embroider the "Horn of Plenty", the stems and the pumpkins with a stem stitch. Flowers and petals: insert needle from the back into the large holes and pull threads to the points as shown. Alternate the colours of the threads: orange, dark yellow and autumn green.

Fill in the pumpkins with pastel pencils in the tints orange, green and dark yellow; the "Horn" with brownish colours.

F2. see F1.

F3. see F1.

F4. see F1.

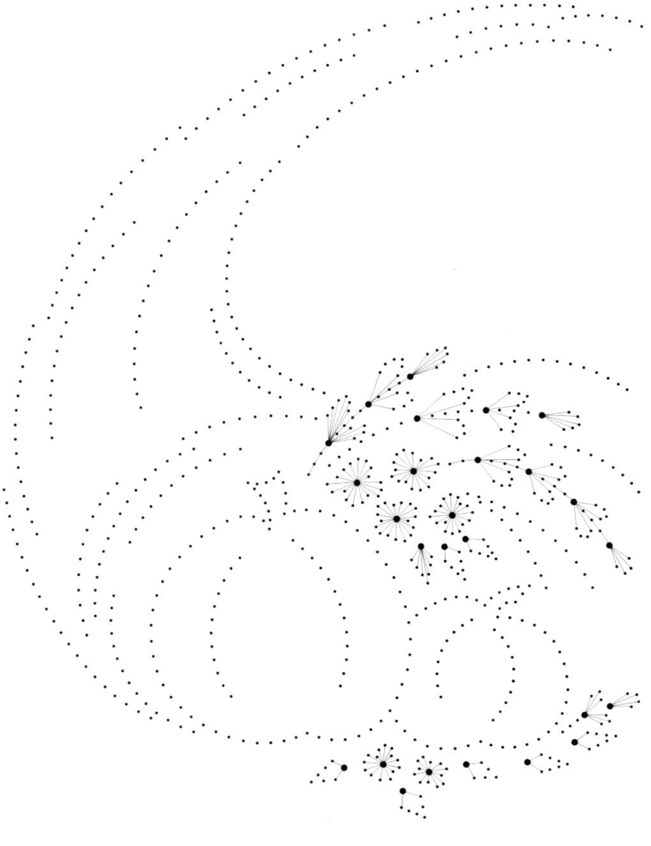

F1

INSTRUCTIONS ON PAGE 26

HAPPY THANKSGIVING
HAPPY
AUTUMN

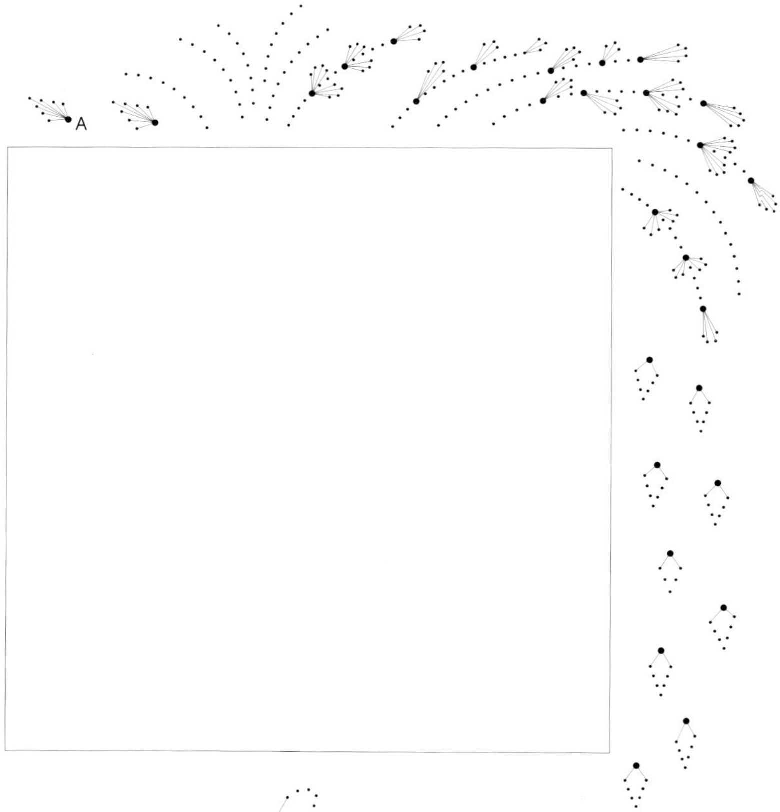

F2

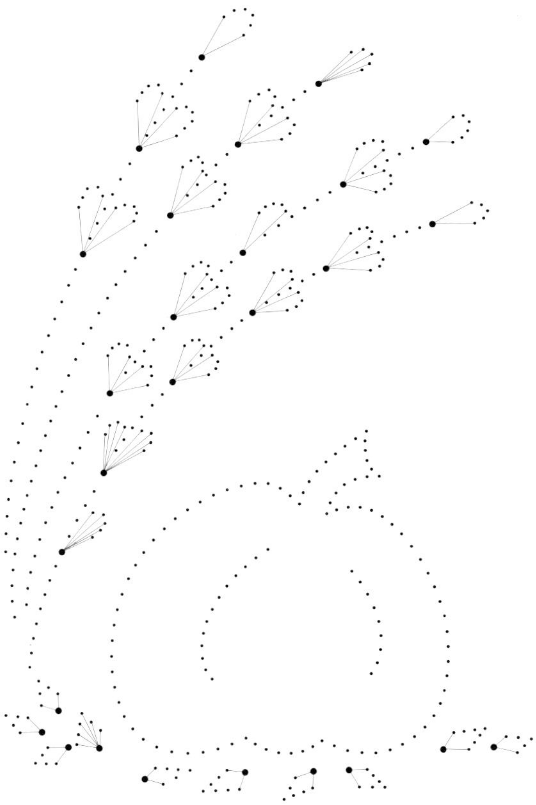

F4

F3

F5. Berries: insert needle from the back at A and pull threads to all points round.

F5

F6. see F1.

F7. Pull the threads from hole to hole. Draw them really tight.

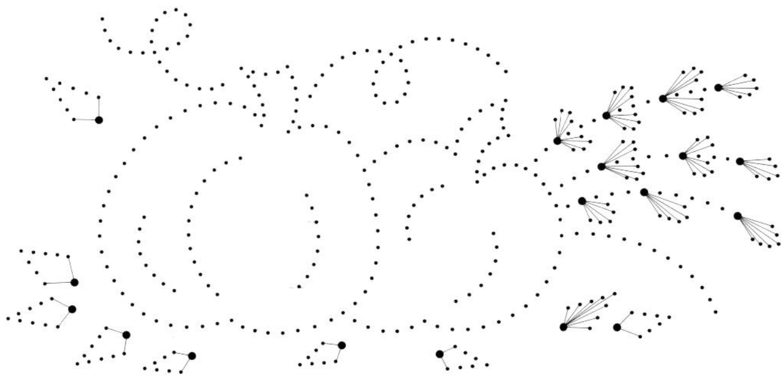

F6

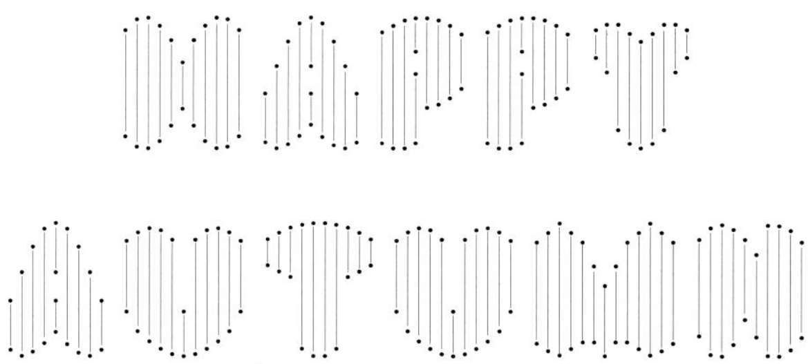

F7a

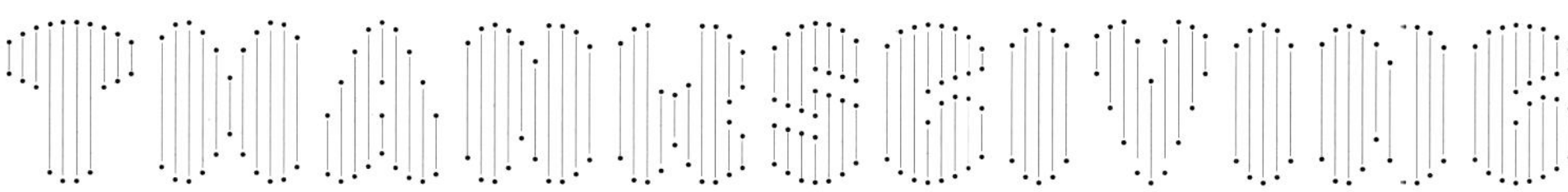

F7b

INSTRUCTIONS ON PAGE 20

Our Trip

Wedding and Thank You cards

Stencil used: Victorian

G1. Insert needle from the back at 1 and pull thread to 2. Go along the back to 3 and pull thread to 4, etc., until you have worked around the ring. Two threads will stick out from each hole.

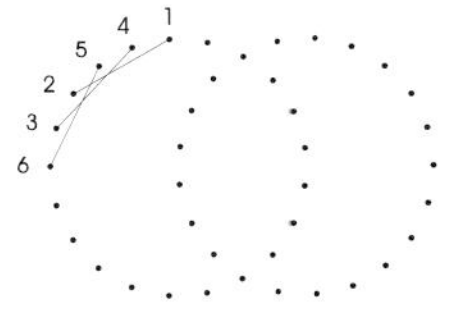

G1

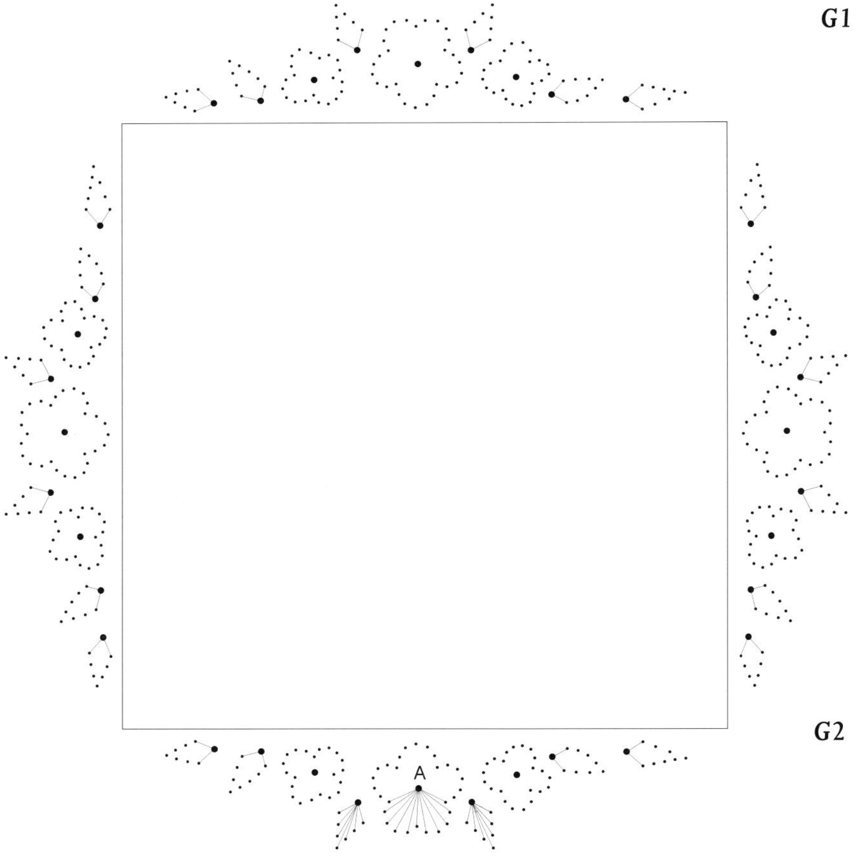

G2

G2. Insert needle from the back in the central hole and pull threads to all points as shown. Make the petals in the same way.

G3. Wings: insert needle from the back at 1 and pull thread to 2. Go along the back to 3 and pull the thread to 4. Go along the back to 5 and pull thread to 6 etc., until you are back at 1. Outline of pigeon and ribbon: in stem stitch.

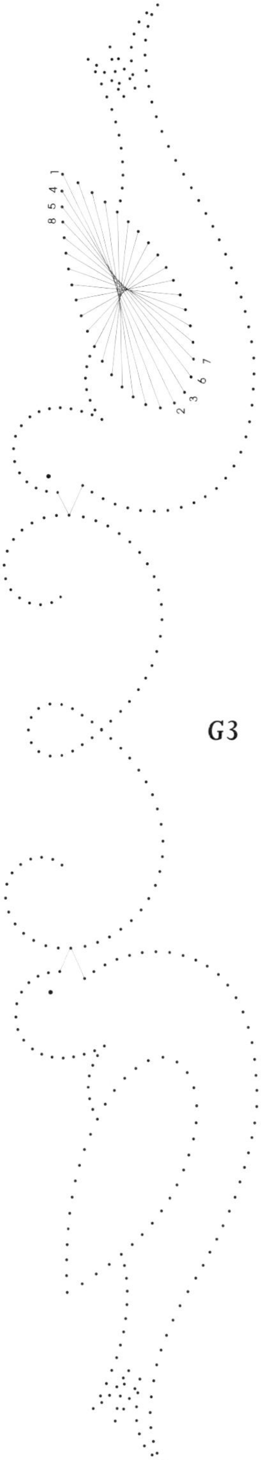

G3

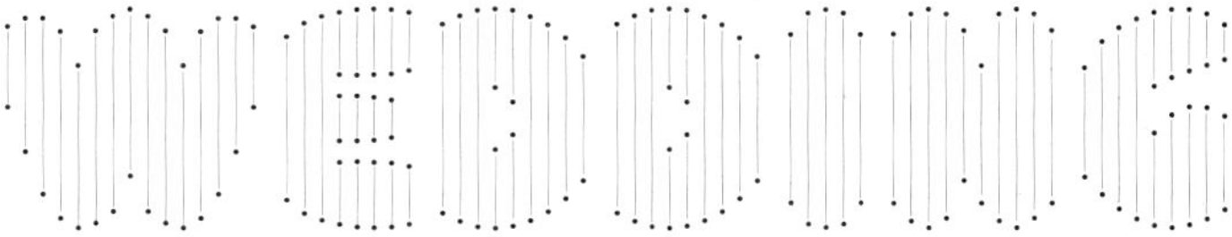

G4

G4. Pull the threads from hole to hole. Draw the threads really tight.

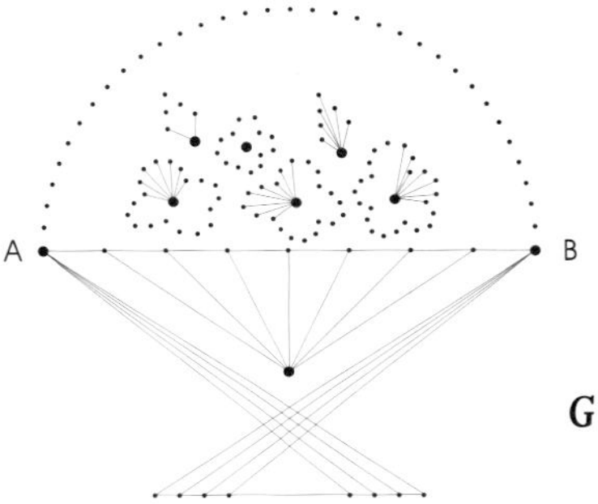

G5

G5. Insert needle from the back at A and pull threads as shown. Repeat this from B and C.

Embroider the hinge in stem stitch. Flowers and petals: see G2.

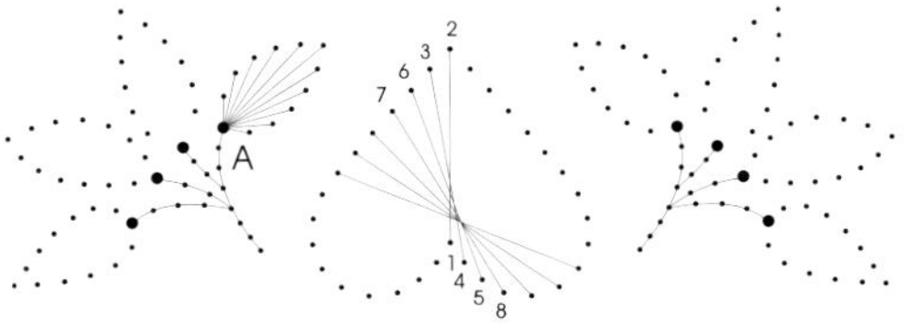

G6. Insert needle from the back at 1 and pull thread to 2. Go along the back to 3 and pull needle to 4, etc., until you have worked around the heart and are back at 1. Stems in stem stitch. Petals see: see G2.

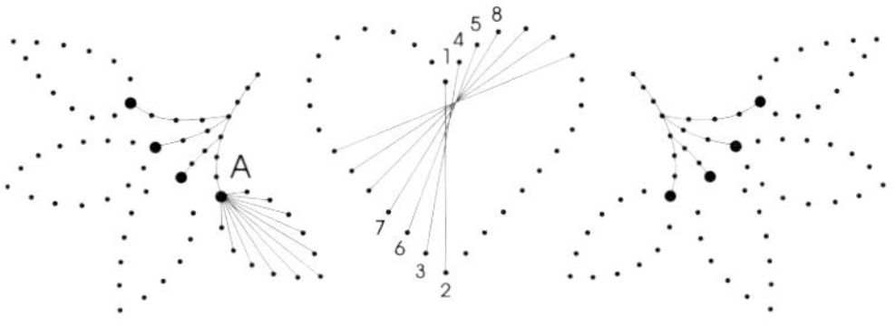

G6

G7. Embroider the text in stem stitch, skipping only one hole.

G7

INSTRUCTIONS ON PAGE 32

Thank You
7-6-
196
MARY AND TOM'S
WEDDING

Christmas cards and Christmas page

Stencil used: Romantic

H1. Embroider the pot by pulling threads as shown. Embroider the outline of the tree with a stem stitch. Christmas tree decoration: insert needle from the back at 1 and pull thread to 2. Go along the back to 3 and pull thread to 4., etc. until you have worked around the circle and two threads stick out of each hole. Star: insert needle from back into central point and pull threads to all points around.

H2. Embroider halo, hair, mouth and collar with stem stitch. Leaf-shaped collar: insert needle from the back into hole (bold type) and pull threads to all points as shown. Make the eyes with a bead or by means of a knot in the thread.

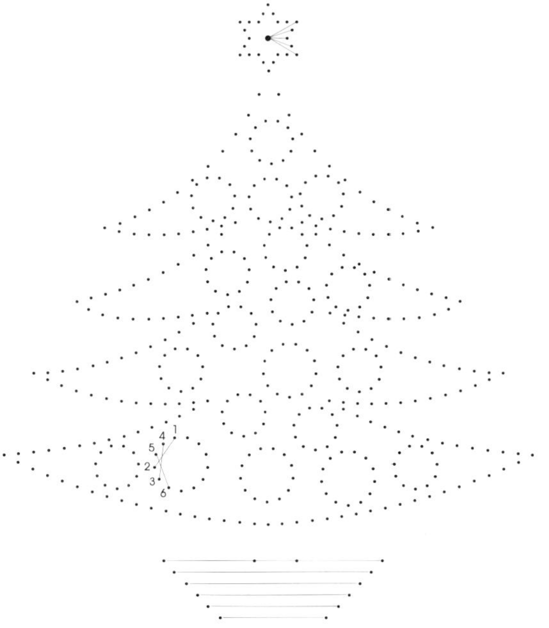

H1

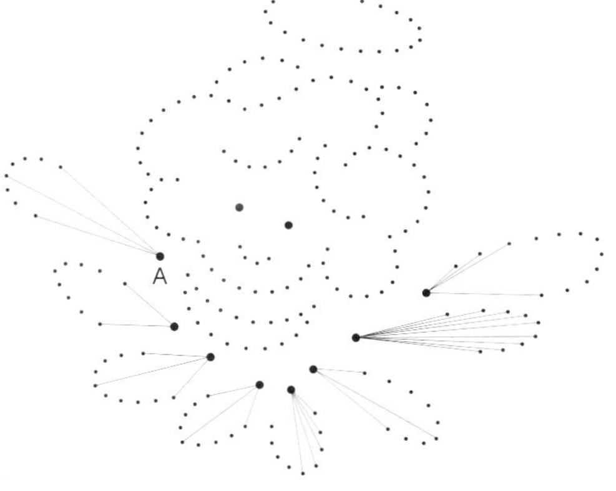

H2

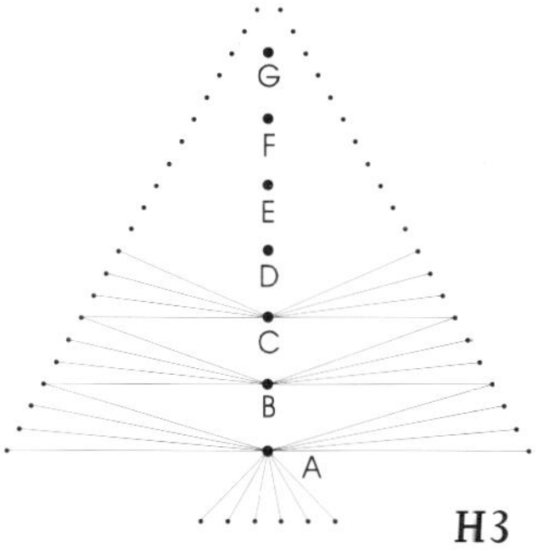

H3

H3. Insert needle from back at A and pull threads to all points as shown. Repeat this from B, C, D, etc.

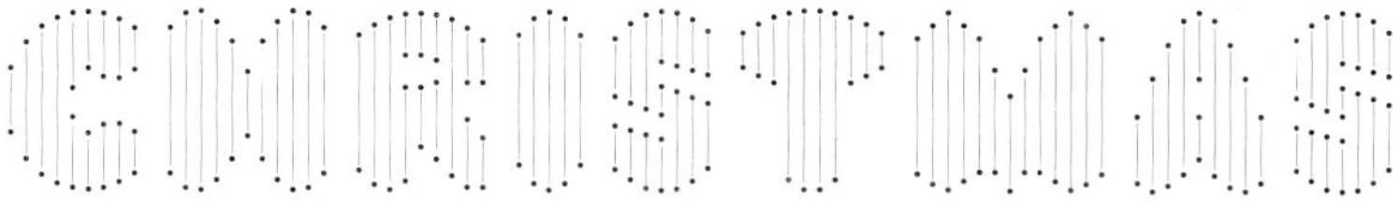

H4x

CHRISTMAS: pull the threads of the letters from hole to hole. Draw the threads really tight.

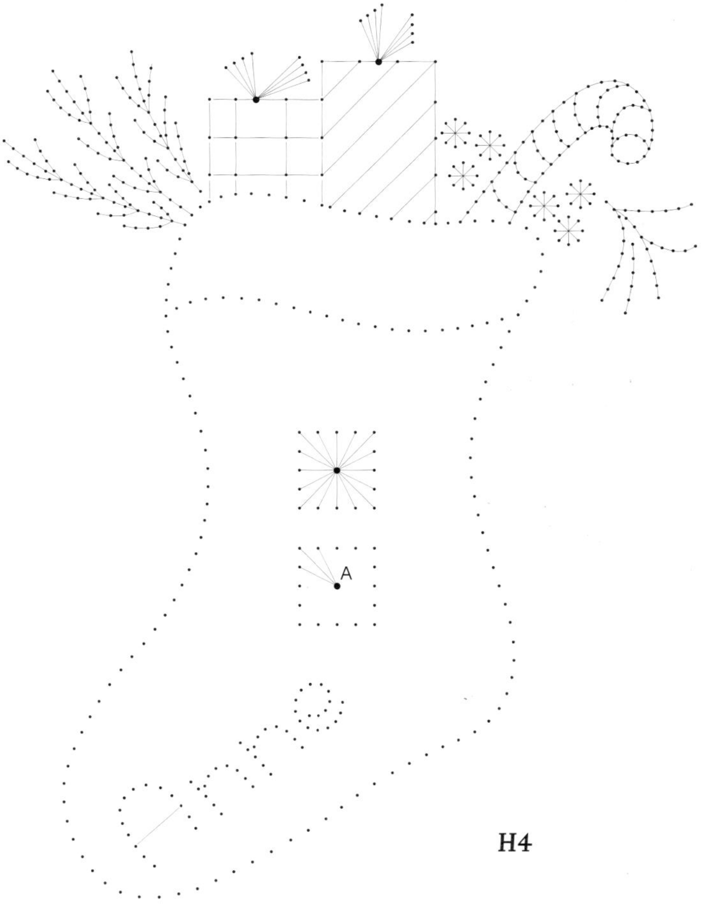

H4

H4. Embroider the outline of the sock, the stems, and the letters "Anne" with stem stitch. Pull the straight threads of the berries, the parcels and the ribbons on the parcels. Squares: insert needle from the back at A and pull threads to points around.

Anne

A Baby Boy is a Joy

Stencil used: Geometrical

I1. Insert needle from the back at A and pull threads to the points as shown. Pull the straight thread below the hat. Make the face, the mouth and the hands in stem stitch. Pull the straight lines of the body. Crosses: insert needle from the back at 1 and pull thread to 2. Go along the back to 3 and pull thread to 4, etc., until you have worked round the cross.

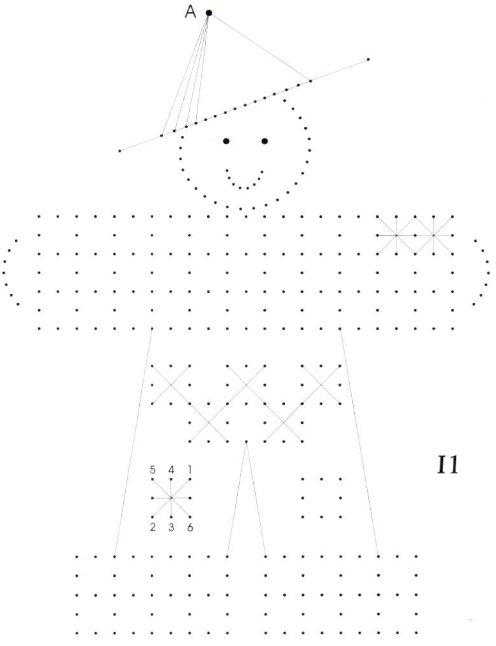

I1

I2. Insert needle from the back into central hole and from here pull threads to the points as shown.

I2

INSTRUCTIONS ON PAGE 36

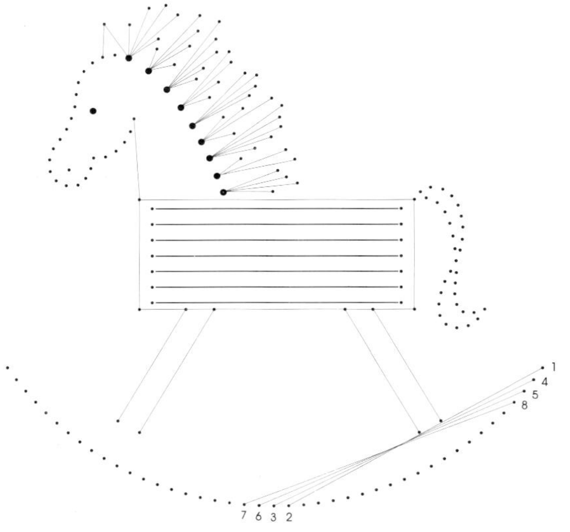

I3

I3. Make the outline of the head and tail in stem stitch. Pull all straight threads as shown. Underframe: insert needle from back at 1 and pull needle to 2. Go along back to 3 and pull needle to 4, etc.

I4. Insert needle from the back at A and pull threads to the points as shown.

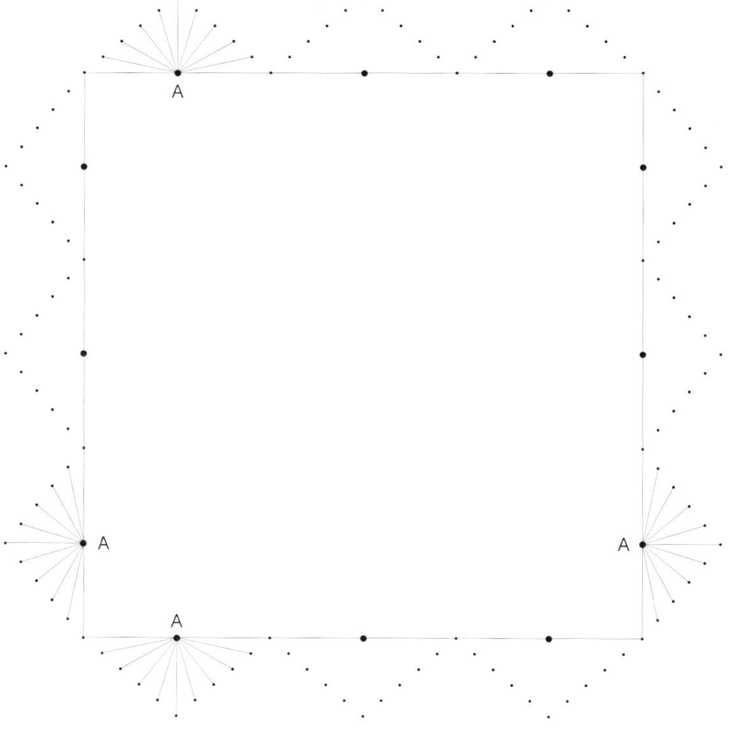

I4

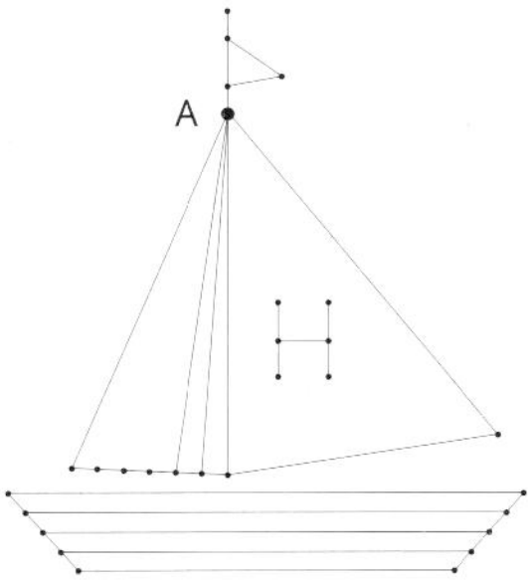

I5

I5. Insert needle from the back at A and pull threads to the points as shown. Pull the straight threads of the boat, sails and mast.

I6. Insert needle from the back at A and pull threads to the points as shown. Pull all straight threads. Insert needle from the back at 1 and pull thread to 2. Go along back to 3 and pull thread to 4, etc., until you have worked around the triangle. Make the face and mouth in stem stitch and the eyes with a bead or a knot in the thread.

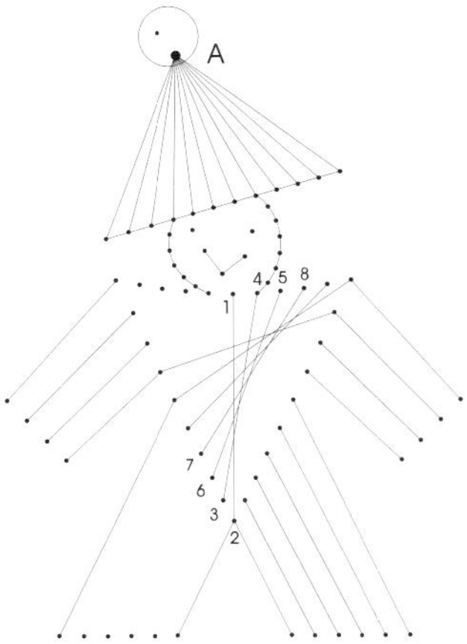

I6

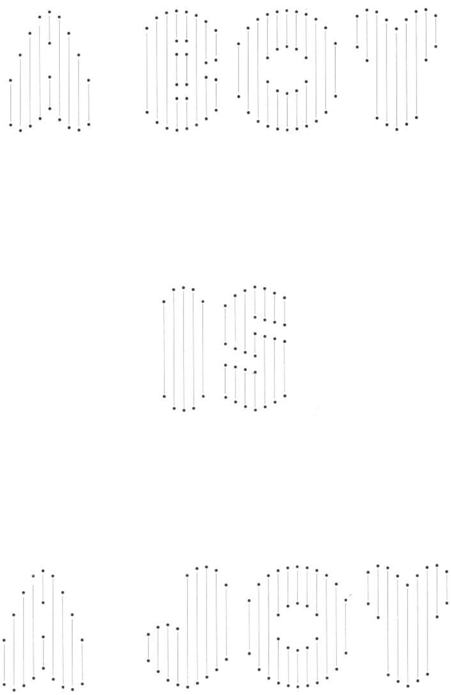

I7

I7. Pull the threads from hole to hole. Draw the threads really tight.

Great

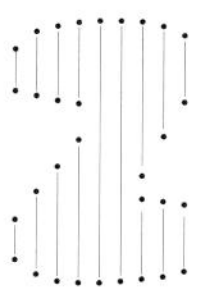

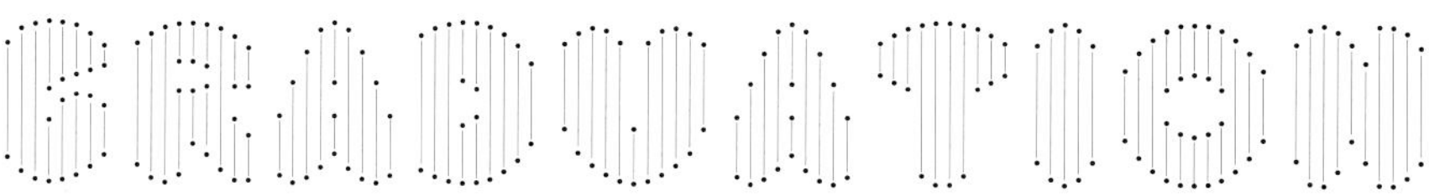

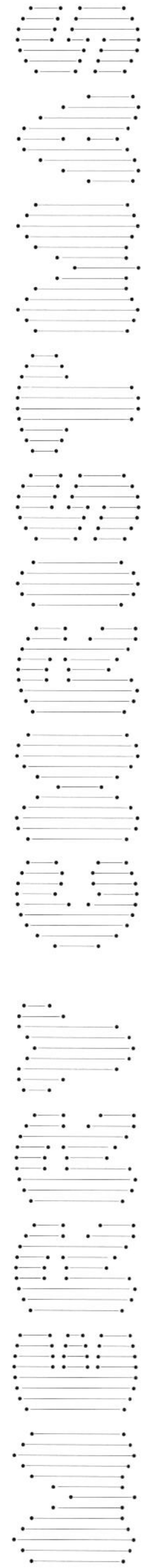

INSTRUCTIONS ON PAGE 39

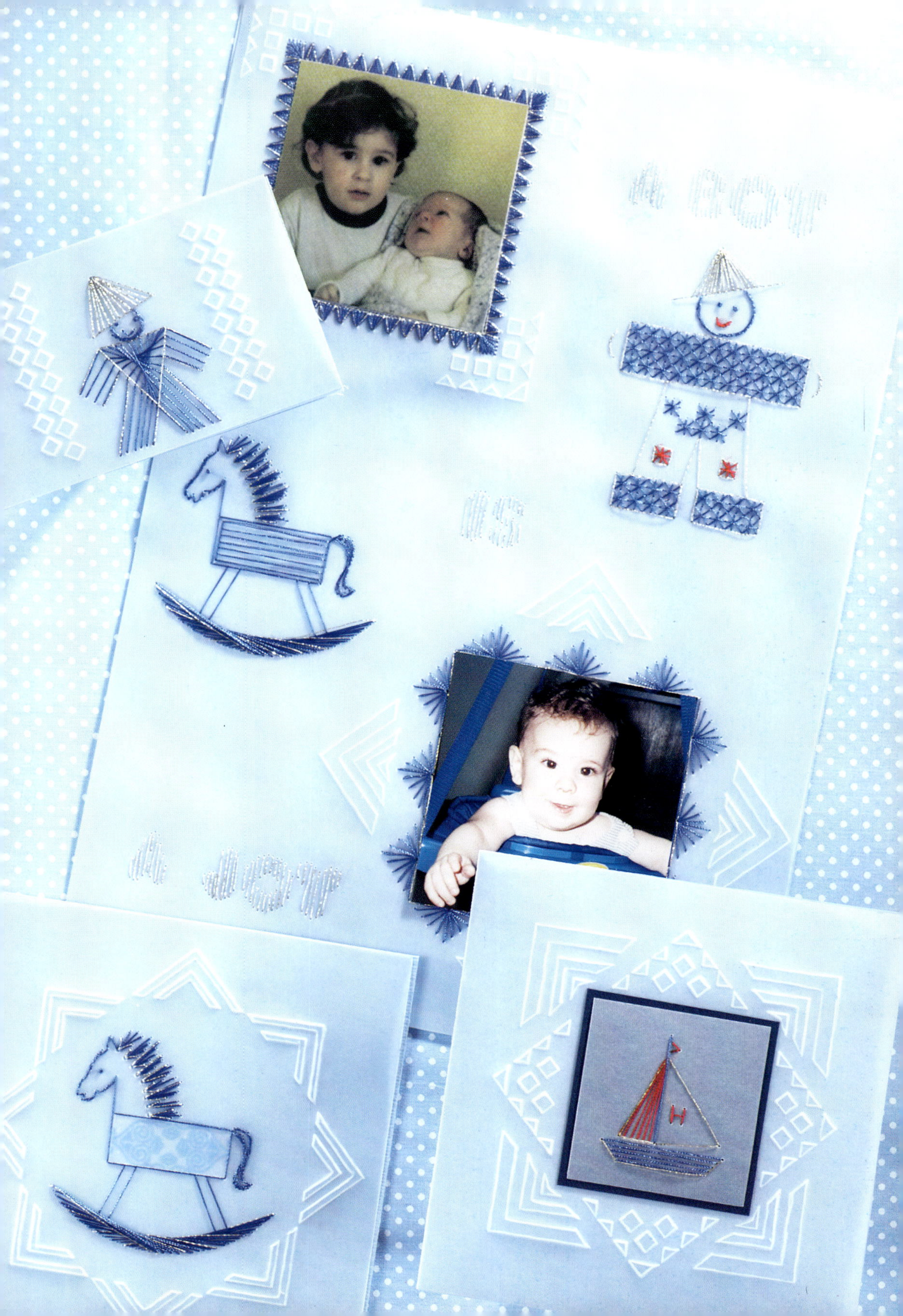

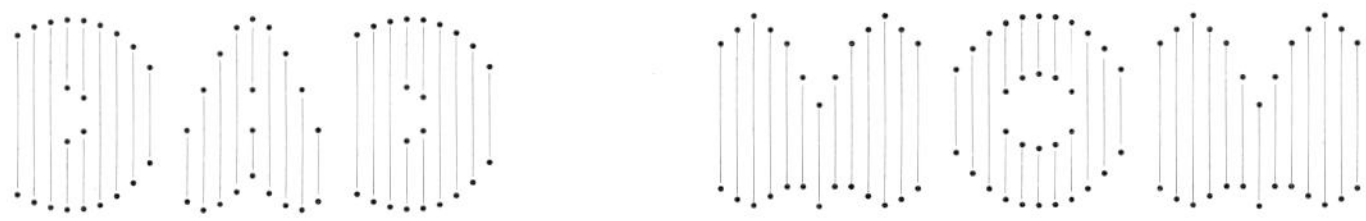

Small

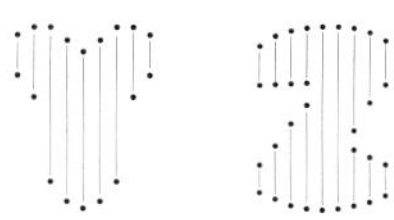

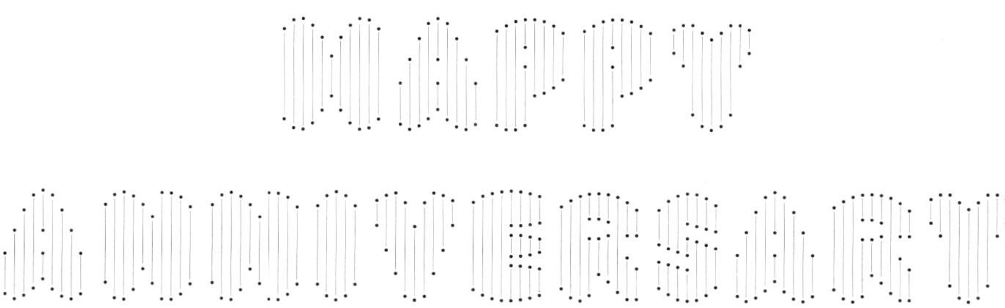

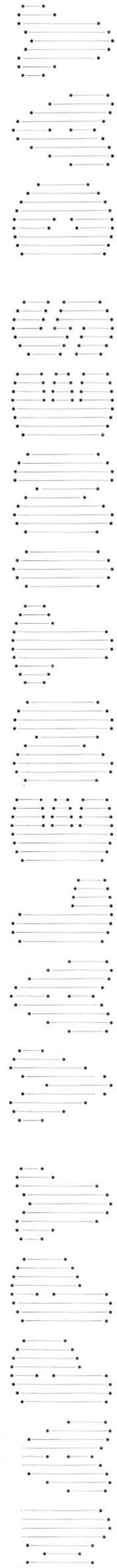

HAPPY BIRTHDAY
WEDDING
GRANDMA
GRANDPA
A BABY GIRL
A BABY BOY
WHAT FUN
HAPPY AUTUMN
OUR DEAREST

OUR TRIP CHEESE

A SPECIAL PERSON

HAPPY THANKSGIVING

GOD BLESS AMERICA

More available

ISBN 90 213 31772

ISBN 90 384 1591 5

ISBN 90 213 3178 0